8 WISE WAYS

12 WEEK JOURNAL

8 WISE WAYS

12 WEEK JOURNAL

Kim Rutherford

That Guy's House

London

8 Wise Ways 12 Week Journal

The information given in this book should not be treated as a substitute for professional medical advice. Always consult a medical practitioner. Although the author and publisher have made every effort to ensure that the information in this book was correct at press time, the author and publisher do not assume and hereby disclaim any liability to any party for any loss, damage, or disruption caused by errors or omissions, whether such errors or omissions result from negligence, accident, or any other cause.

Copyright © Kim Rutherford, 2021

All rights reserved. No part of this book may be reproduced in any form, including photocopying and recording, without permission in writing from the publisher, except by a reviewer who may quote brief pages in review.

The book information is catalogued as follows;
Author Name(s): Kim Rutherford
Title: 8 Wise Ways 12 Week Journal
Description; First Edition

1st Edition, 2021

Book Design by Leah Kent

ISBN (paperback) 978-1-913479-94-7

Published by That Guy's House
www.ThatGuysHouse.com

Take back control of your mental wellness for a healthier and happier life.

This Journal can be used with '8Wise Ways to a Healthier and Happier Life', by Kim Rutherford, 2021, publisher: That Guy's House or as a standalone Journal to help you manage the chaos, challenges and traumas of life through accessing all areas of your wellness spectrum effectively and positively.

"The ability to successfully handle life's stresses and adapt to change and difficult situations requires you to accept your emotions and work through them in a positive and healthy way."

An Introduction to 8Wise™

8Wise™ looks at your wellness and wellbeing through four core dimensions:

1. **Foundation Dimension** for strong health and wellbeing through Physical wellness and Emotional wellness.

2. **Internal Dimension** for achieving self-acceptance through Spiritual and Intellectual wellness.

3. **External Dimension** for interacting with the world positively and effectively through Environmental wellness is Social wellness.

4. **Lifestyle Dimension** for creating the fulfilling life you want for yourself supported by Occupational wellness and Financial wellness.

8Wise™ can help you to assess your current wellness levels, set realistic goals for a healthier happier mind.

8Wise™ helps you to develop the tools to manage your stress and life challenges to protect your longer term mental and physical health for a happier, healthier and fulfilling life.

"To achieve optimal mental and physical health, you must balance exercise, sleep habits, nutrition and listening to your body when it is trying to tell you something."

THE EIGHT ELEMENTS
OF WELLNESS

The Eight Elements of Wellness

Emotional Wellness
Have a positive attitude, high self-esteem, a strong sense of self, and the ability to recognise and share a wide range of feelings with others in a constructive way

Physical Wellness
Take care of your body for optimal health and functioning

Spiritual Wellness
Find meaning in life events, demonstrate individual's purpose, and live a life that reflects your values and beliefs

Intellectual Wellness
Learn more, be open to new ideas, be creative, think critically, and seek out new challenges

Environmental Wellness
Be aware of the interactions between the environment, community and yourself and behave in ways that care for each of these responsibly

Social Wellness
Build relationships with others, deal with conflict appropriately, and connect to a positive social network

Occupational Wellness
Seek to have a career that is interesting, enjoyable, meaningful and that contributes to the larger society

Financial Wellness
Live within your means and learn to manage your finances for the short and long term.

"Spiritually well people use their own set of values, principles, morals and beliefs to guide their actions and decisions with confidence."

The 8Wise™ Map

Assess yourself against each of the eight elements of wellness to create your 8Wise™ Map (example below)

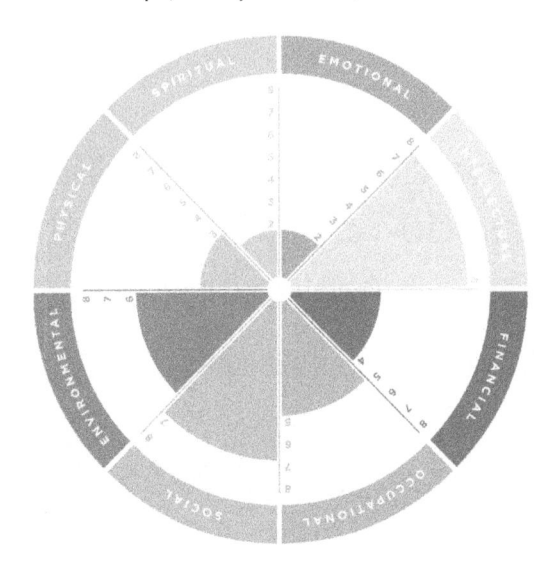

Set yourself three goals to improve your wellness within 12 weeks

Short term goal - Achievable in 4 weeks

Midterm goal - Achievable in 8 weeks

Long term goal - Achievable in 12 weeks

"People that master mental stimulation by stretching their comfort zones and learning about things separate from their normal realm develop better wellness and wellbeing."

Your 8Wise™ Map

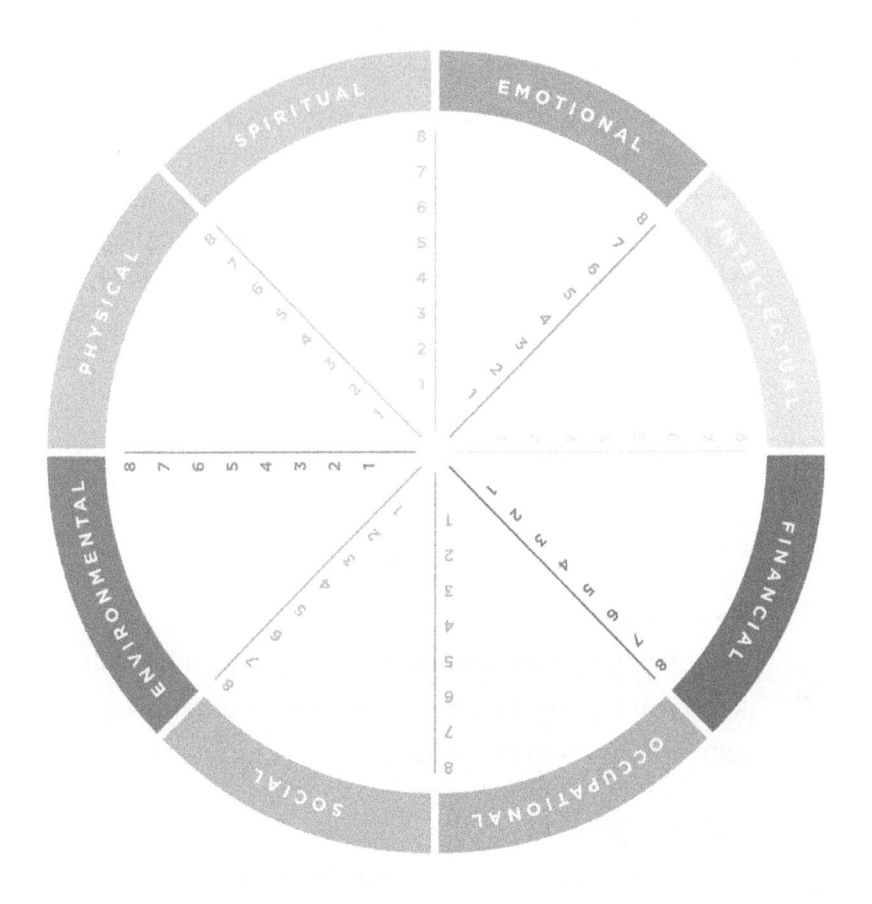

Rate your wellness against each of the wellness elements from 1 to 8 (1 = low, 8 = high) and plot your answer on the diagram above.

Emotional Wellness Tips

1 **Awareness of thoughts and feelings**
Take time to become aware of certain thoughts or triggers that cause these negative emotions

2 **Staying positive**
Noticing how often you think or say negative things is the first step towards having a positive attitude - then work on limiting it

3 **Ask for help**
Seeking support doesn't mean you are weak; it means you are strong enough to take care of your mental health

4 **Keep Boundaries**
Establishing boundaries with people in your life will keep you from feeling overwhelmed by other people's expectations and behaviours

5 **Self Acceptance**
Becoming aware and then learning how to manage negative thoughts and self-talk is key to learning how to accept yourself

Physical Wellness Tips

1 **Sleep**
Your body craves a regular routine especially when it comes to sleep. Create a routine that works for you with the aim of 7-9 hours sleep.

2 **Eating Well**
A routine of eating vegetables, fruits, lean meats and whole grains gives your body the nutrients for better function and balance your mental well-being as well

3 **Physical Exercise**
A routine of daily exercise has both short term and leg term benefits to your wellness and wellbeing, aim for 30 minutes a day of some activity you enjoy

4 **Hygiene**
Hygiene includes both personal care and preventative medical care, so stay clean and fresh daily and don't put off those health checks

5 **Relaxation**
Whether it is getting a massage, staying home with a good book or playing your favourite sport, some "me time" does everyone good.

Notes

Daily Reflection: Week One

Date	M	Tu	W	Th	F	Sa	Su

How is your wellness today?	UP	OK	DOWN
EMOTIONAL			
PHYSICAL			
SPIRITUAL			
INTELLECTUAL			
ENVIRONMENTAL			
SOCIAL			
OCCUPATIONAL			
FINANCIAL			

How have you improved your wellness today?

What are your wellness plans for tomorrow?

Name one positive from today

Notes

Daily Reflection: Week One

Date M Tu W Th F Sa Su

| **How is your wellness today?** | **UP** | **OK** | **DOWN** |

- EMOTIONAL
- PHYSICAL
- SPIRITUAL
- INTELLECTUAL
- ENVIRONMENTAL
- SOCIAL
- OCCUPATIONAL
- FINANCIAL

How have you improved your wellness today?

What are your wellness plans for tomorrow?

Name one positive from today

Notes

Daily Reflection: Week One

Date _____   M Tu W Th F Sa Su

How is your wellness today?	UP	OK	DOWN
EMOTIONAL			
PHYSICAL			
SPIRITUAL			
INTELLECTUAL			
ENVIRONMENTAL			
SOCIAL			
OCCUPATIONAL			
FINANCIAL			

How have you improved your wellness today?

What are your wellness plans for tomorrow?

Name one positive from today

Notes

Daily Reflection: Week One

Date M Tu W Th F Sa Su

How is your wellness today?	UP	OK	DOWN
EMOTIONAL			
PHYSICAL			
SPIRITUAL			
INTELLECTUAL			
ENVIRONMENTAL			
SOCIAL			
OCCUPATIONAL			
FINANCIAL			

How have you improved your wellness today?

What are your wellness plans for tomorrow?

Name one positive from today

Notes

Daily Reflection: Week One

Date _____ M Tu W Th F Sa Su

How is your wellness today?	UP	OK	DOWN
EMOTIONAL			
PHYSICAL			
SPIRITUAL			
INTELLECTUAL			
ENVIRONMENTAL			
SOCIAL			
OCCUPATIONAL			
FINANCIAL			

How have you improved your wellness today?

What are your wellness plans for tomorrow?

Name one positive from today

Notes

Daily Reflection: Week Two

Date   M   Tu   W   Th   F   Sa   Su

How is your wellness today?	UP	OK	DOWN
EMOTIONAL			
PHYSICAL			
SPIRITUAL			
INTELLECTUAL			
ENVIRONMENTAL			
SOCIAL			
OCCUPATIONAL			
FINANCIAL			

How have you improved your wellness today?

What are your wellness plans for tomorrow?

Name one positive from today

Notes

Daily Reflection: Week Two

Date _____   M   Tu   W   Th   F   Sa   Su

How is your wellness today?	UP	OK	DOWN
EMOTIONAL			
PHYSICAL			
SPIRITUAL			
INTELLECTUAL			
ENVIRONMENTAL			
SOCIAL			
OCCUPATIONAL			
FINANCIAL			

How have you improved your wellness today?

What are your wellness plans for tomorrow?

Name one positive from today

Notes

Daily Reflection: Week Two

Date   M   Tu   W   Th   F   Sa   Su

How is your wellness today?	UP	OK	DOWN
EMOTIONAL			
PHYSICAL			
SPIRITUAL			
INTELLECTUAL			
ENVIRONMENTAL			
SOCIAL			
OCCUPATIONAL			
FINANCIAL			

How have you improved your wellness today?

What are your wellness plans for tomorrow?

Name one positive from today

Notes

Daily Reflection: Week Two

Date M Tu W Th F Sa Su

How is your wellness today?	UP	OK	DOWN
EMOTIONAL			
PHYSICAL			
SPIRITUAL			
INTELLECTUAL			
ENVIRONMENTAL			
SOCIAL			
OCCUPATIONAL			
FINANCIAL			

How have you improved your wellness today?

What are your wellness plans for tomorrow?

Name one positive from today

Notes

Daily Reflection: Week Three

Date   M   Tu   W   Th   F   Sa   Su

How is your wellness today?	UP	OK	DOWN
EMOTIONAL			
PHYSICAL			
SPIRITUAL			
INTELLECTUAL			
ENVIRONMENTAL			
SOCIAL			
OCCUPATIONAL			
FINANCIAL			

How have you improved your wellness today?

What are your wellness plans for tomorrow?

Name one positive from today

Notes

Daily Reflection: Week Three

Date   M   Tu   W   Th   F   Sa   Su

How is your wellness today?	UP	OK	DOWN
EMOTIONAL			
PHYSICAL			
SPIRITUAL			
INTELLECTUAL			
ENVIRONMENTAL			
SOCIAL			
OCCUPATIONAL			
FINANCIAL			

How have you improved your wellness today?

What are your wellness plans for tomorrow?

Name one positive from today

Notes

Daily Reflection: Week Three

Date   M   Tu   W   Th   F   Sa   Su

How is your wellness today?	UP	OK	DOWN
EMOTIONAL			
PHYSICAL			
SPIRITUAL			
INTELLECTUAL			
ENVIRONMENTAL			
SOCIAL			
OCCUPATIONAL			
FINANCIAL			

How have you improved your wellness today?

What are your wellness plans for tomorrow?

Name one positive from today

Notes

Daily Reflection: Week Three

Date　　　　　　　　　　M Tu W Th F Sa Su

How is your wellness today?	UP	OK	DOWN
EMOTIONAL			
PHYSICAL			
SPIRITUAL			
INTELLECTUAL			
ENVIRONMENTAL			
SOCIAL			
OCCUPATIONAL			
FINANCIAL			

How have you improved your wellness today?

What are your wellness plans for tomorrow?

Name one positive from today

Notes

Daily Reflection: Week Three

Date _____   M   Tu   W   Th   F   Sa   Su

How is your wellness today?	UP	OK	DOWN
EMOTIONAL			
PHYSICAL			
SPIRITUAL			
INTELLECTUAL			
ENVIRONMENTAL			
SOCIAL			
OCCUPATIONAL			
FINANCIAL			

How have you improved your wellness today?

What are your wellness plans for tomorrow?

Name one positive from today

Notes

Daily Reflection: Week Three

Date   M   Tu   W   Th   F   Sa   Su

How is your wellness today?	UP	OK	DOWN
EMOTIONAL			
PHYSICAL			
SPIRITUAL			
INTELLECTUAL			
ENVIRONMENTAL			
SOCIAL			
OCCUPATIONAL			
FINANCIAL			

How have you improved your wellness today?

What are your wellness plans for tomorrow?

Name one positive from today

Notes

Daily Reflection: Week Four

Date M Tu W Th F Sa Su

How is your wellness today?	UP	OK	DOWN
EMOTIONAL			
PHYSICAL			
SPIRITUAL			
INTELLECTUAL			
ENVIRONMENTAL			
SOCIAL			
OCCUPATIONAL			
FINANCIAL			

How have you improved your wellness today?

What are your wellness plans for tomorrow?

Name one positive from today

Notes

Daily Reflection: Week Four

Date   M   Tu   W   Th   F   Sa   Su

How is your wellness today?	UP	OK	DOWN
EMOTIONAL			
PHYSICAL			
SPIRITUAL			
INTELLECTUAL			
ENVIRONMENTAL			
SOCIAL			
OCCUPATIONAL			
FINANCIAL			

How have you improved your wellness today?

What are your wellness plans for tomorrow?

Name one positive from today

Notes

Daily Reflection: Week Four

Date M Tu W Th F Sa Su

How is your wellness today?	UP	OK	DOWN
EMOTIONAL			
PHYSICAL			
SPIRITUAL			
INTELLECTUAL			
ENVIRONMENTAL			
SOCIAL			
OCCUPATIONAL			
FINANCIAL			

How have you improved your wellness today?

What are your wellness plans for tomorrow?

Name one positive from today

Notes

Daily Reflection: Week Four

Date   M Tu W Th F Sa Su

How is your wellness today?	UP	OK	DOWN
EMOTIONAL			
PHYSICAL			
SPIRITUAL			
INTELLECTUAL			
ENVIRONMENTAL			
SOCIAL			
OCCUPATIONAL			
FINANCIAL			

How have you improved your wellness today?

What are your wellness plans for tomorrow?

Name one positive from today

Notes

Daily Reflection: Week Four

Date   M   Tu   W   Th   F   Sa   Su

How is your wellness today?	UP	OK	DOWN
EMOTIONAL			
PHYSICAL			
SPIRITUAL			
INTELLECTUAL			
ENVIRONMENTAL			
SOCIAL			
OCCUPATIONAL			
FINANCIAL			

How have you improved your wellness today?

What are your wellness plans for tomorrow?

Name one positive from today

Notes

Daily Reflection: Week Four

Date _____   M Tu W Th F Sa Su

How is your wellness today?	UP	OK	DOWN
EMOTIONAL			
PHYSICAL			
SPIRITUAL			
INTELLECTUAL			
ENVIRONMENTAL			
SOCIAL			
OCCUPATIONAL			
FINANCIAL			

How have you improved your wellness today?

What are your wellness plans for tomorrow?

Name one positive from today

Notes

Daily Reflection: Week Four

Date   M   Tu   W   Th   F   Sa   Su

How is your wellness today?	UP	OK	DOWN
EMOTIONAL			
PHYSICAL			
SPIRITUAL			
INTELLECTUAL			
ENVIRONMENTAL			
SOCIAL			
OCCUPATIONAL			
FINANCIAL			

How have you improved your wellness today?

What are your wellness plans for tomorrow?

Name one positive from today

Month One Review

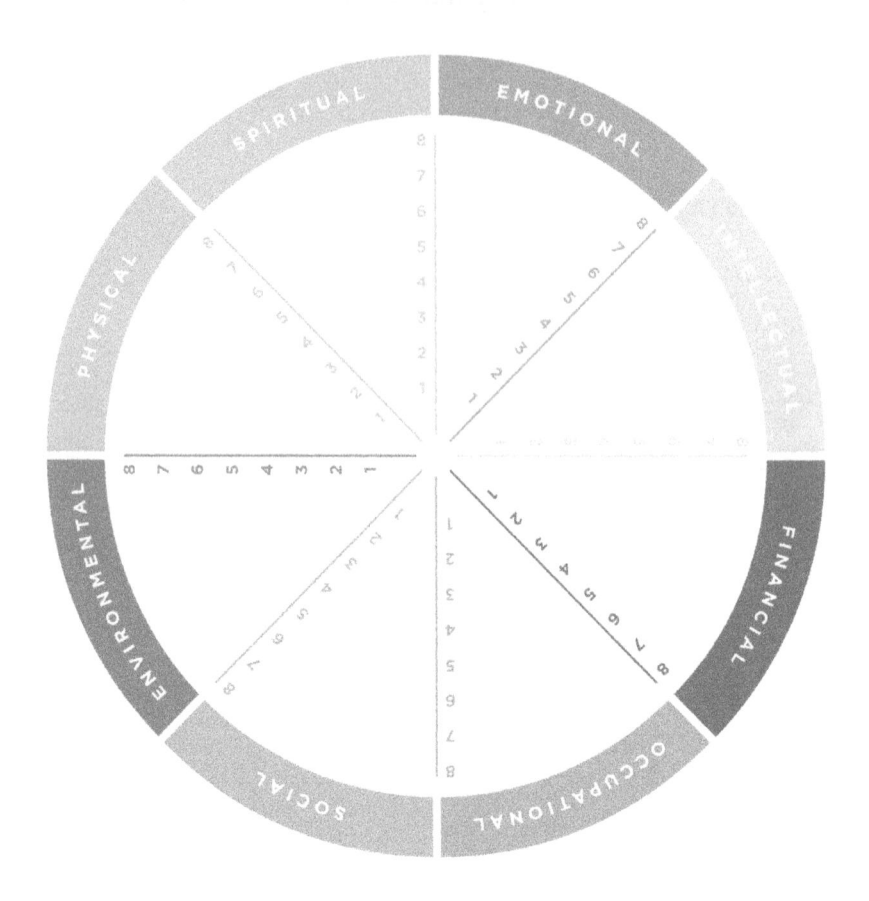

Reassess yourself against the eight wellness elements. Have there been any changes?

Month One Self Reflection

What went well this month?

What did not go well this month?

What have you learnt from the past month?

Review your goals *(goals can be changed and adapted if need be)*	**On Track**	**On Hold**	**Problem**
SHORT TERM GOAL			
MIDTERM GOAL			
LONG TERM GOAL			

Spiritual Wellness Tips

1 **Values and Beliefs**
Understand yourself, what are the values and core beliefs the drive you. How do they reflect in your behaviours?

2 **Purpose**
Reflect on your purpose, how does it align with your values, beliefs and behaviours. reflect on you identify and feel confident in your choices.

3 **Self-Acceptance**
Learn to accept yourself, for who you are not who you wish you were. You are unique be confident in who you are and the choices you make in life

4 **Gratitude**
Being grateful for what you have in life that brings you joy, and peace will help bring calm, clarity and inner strength.

5 **Be Mindful**
Living in the moment teaches you to appreciate life and all its everyday pleasures and curiosities.

Intellectual Wellness Tips

1 **Read for fun**
Reading things you enjoy improves your intellect by stretching your mind to think about new things.

2 **Podcasts**
Podcasts are also excellent ways to learn about new topics you may be interested in

3 **Learn a new skill**
No matter what it is, learning a new skill is a fun and interactive way to improve your intellectual intelligence

4 **Time Management**
Poor time management can lead to increased stress, affects all wellness areas. Being organised allows your mind to work more efficiently and effectively

5 **Create**
Similar to the positive effects of reading, being creative is known to improve memory retention as well as emotional stability

Notes

Daily Reflection: Week Five

Date　　　　　　　　　　　　M　Tu　W　Th　F　Sa　Su

How is your wellness today?	UP	OK	DOWN
EMOTIONAL			
PHYSICAL			
SPIRITUAL			
INTELLECTUAL			
ENVIRONMENTAL			
SOCIAL			
OCCUPATIONAL			
FINANCIAL			

How have you improved your wellness today?

What are your wellness plans for tomorrow?

Name one positive from today

Notes

Daily Reflection: Week Five

Date   M   Tu   W   Th   F   Sa   Su

How is your wellness today?	UP	OK	DOWN
EMOTIONAL			
PHYSICAL			
SPIRITUAL			
INTELLECTUAL			
ENVIRONMENTAL			
SOCIAL			
OCCUPATIONAL			
FINANCIAL			

How have you improved your wellness today?

What are your wellness plans for tomorrow?

Name one positive from today

Notes

Daily Reflection: Week Five

Date M Tu W Th F Sa Su

How is your wellness today?	UP	OK	DOWN
EMOTIONAL			
PHYSICAL			
SPIRITUAL			
INTELLECTUAL			
ENVIRONMENTAL			
SOCIAL			
OCCUPATIONAL			
FINANCIAL			

How have you improved your wellness today?

What are your wellness plans for tomorrow?

Name one positive from today

Notes

Daily Reflection: Week Five

Date   M Tu W Th F Sa Su

How is your wellness today?	UP	OK	DOWN
EMOTIONAL			
PHYSICAL			
SPIRITUAL			
INTELLECTUAL			
ENVIRONMENTAL			
SOCIAL			
OCCUPATIONAL			
FINANCIAL			

How have you improved your wellness today?

What are your wellness plans for tomorrow?

Name one positive from today

Notes

Daily Reflection: Week Five

Date   M   Tu   W   Th   F   Sa   Su

How is your wellness today?	UP	OK	DOWN
EMOTIONAL			
PHYSICAL			
SPIRITUAL			
INTELLECTUAL			
ENVIRONMENTAL			
SOCIAL			
OCCUPATIONAL			
FINANCIAL			

How have you improved your wellness today?

What are your wellness plans for tomorrow?

Name one positive from today

Notes

Daily Reflection: Week Five

Date M Tu W Th F Sa Su

How is your wellness today?	UP	OK	DOWN
EMOTIONAL			
PHYSICAL			
SPIRITUAL			
INTELLECTUAL			
ENVIRONMENTAL			
SOCIAL			
OCCUPATIONAL			
FINANCIAL			

How have you improved your wellness today?

What are your wellness plans for tomorrow?

Name one positive from today

Notes

Daily Reflection: Week Five

Date　　　　　　　　　　　M　Tu　W　Th　F　Sa　Su

How is your wellness today?	UP	OK	DOWN
EMOTIONAL			
PHYSICAL			
SPIRITUAL			
INTELLECTUAL			
ENVIRONMENTAL			
SOCIAL			
OCCUPATIONAL			
FINANCIAL			

How have you improved your wellness today?

What are your wellness plans for tomorrow?

Name one positive from today

Notes

Daily Reflection: Week Six

Date M Tu W Th F Sa Su

How is your wellness today?	UP	OK	DOWN
EMOTIONAL			
PHYSICAL			
SPIRITUAL			
INTELLECTUAL			
ENVIRONMENTAL			
SOCIAL			
OCCUPATIONAL			
FINANCIAL			

How have you improved your wellness today?

What are your wellness plans for tomorrow?

Name one positive from today

Notes

Daily Reflection: Week Six

Date M Tu W Th F Sa Su

How is your wellness today?	UP	OK	DOWN
EMOTIONAL			
PHYSICAL			
SPIRITUAL			
INTELLECTUAL			
ENVIRONMENTAL			
SOCIAL			
OCCUPATIONAL			
FINANCIAL			

How have you improved your wellness today?

What are your wellness plans for tomorrow?

Name one positive from today

Notes

Daily Reflection: Week Six

Date   M   Tu   W   Th   F   Sa   Su

How is your wellness today?	UP	OK	DOWN
EMOTIONAL			
PHYSICAL			
SPIRITUAL			
INTELLECTUAL			
ENVIRONMENTAL			
SOCIAL			
OCCUPATIONAL			
FINANCIAL			

How have you improved your wellness today?

What are your wellness plans for tomorrow?

Name one positive from today

Notes

Daily Reflection: Week Six

Date   M   Tu   W   Th   F   Sa   Su

How is your wellness today?	UP	OK	DOWN
EMOTIONAL			
PHYSICAL			
SPIRITUAL			
INTELLECTUAL			
ENVIRONMENTAL			
SOCIAL			
OCCUPATIONAL			
FINANCIAL			

How have you improved your wellness today?

What are your wellness plans for tomorrow?

Name one positive from today

Notes

Daily Reflection: Week Six

Date M Tu W Th F Sa Su

How is your wellness today?	UP	OK	DOWN
EMOTIONAL			
PHYSICAL			
SPIRITUAL			
INTELLECTUAL			
ENVIRONMENTAL			
SOCIAL			
OCCUPATIONAL			
FINANCIAL			

How have you improved your wellness today?

What are your wellness plans for tomorrow?

Name one positive from today

Notes

Daily Reflection: Week Six

Date   M Tu W Th F Sa Su

How is your wellness today?	UP	OK	DOWN
EMOTIONAL			
PHYSICAL			
SPIRITUAL			
INTELLECTUAL			
ENVIRONMENTAL			
SOCIAL			
OCCUPATIONAL			
FINANCIAL			

How have you improved your wellness today?

What are your wellness plans for tomorrow?

Name one positive from today

Notes

Daily Reflection: Week Six

Date   M   Tu   W   Th   F   Sa   Su

How is your wellness today?	UP	OK	DOWN
EMOTIONAL			
PHYSICAL			
SPIRITUAL			
INTELLECTUAL			
ENVIRONMENTAL			
SOCIAL			
OCCUPATIONAL			
FINANCIAL			

How have you improved your wellness today?

What are your wellness plans for tomorrow?

Name one positive from today

Notes

Daily Reflection: Week Seven

Date   M Tu W Th F Sa Su

How is your wellness today?	UP	OK	DOWN
EMOTIONAL			
PHYSICAL			
SPIRITUAL			
INTELLECTUAL			
ENVIRONMENTAL			
SOCIAL			
OCCUPATIONAL			
FINANCIAL			

How have you improved your wellness today?

What are your wellness plans for tomorrow?

Name one positive from today

Notes

Daily Reflection: Week Seven

Date　　　　　　　　　　　M　Tu　W　Th　F　Sa　Su

How is your wellness today?	UP	OK	DOWN
EMOTIONAL			
PHYSICAL			
SPIRITUAL			
INTELLECTUAL			
ENVIRONMENTAL			
SOCIAL			
OCCUPATIONAL			
FINANCIAL			

How have you improved your wellness today?

What are your wellness plans for tomorrow?

Name one positive from today

Notes

Daily Reflection: Week Seven

Date M Tu W Th F Sa Su

How is your wellness today?	UP	OK	DOWN
EMOTIONAL			
PHYSICAL			
SPIRITUAL			
INTELLECTUAL			
ENVIRONMENTAL			
SOCIAL			
OCCUPATIONAL			
FINANCIAL			

How have you improved your wellness today?

What are your wellness plans for tomorrow?

Name one positive from today

Notes

Daily Reflection: Week Seven

Date　　　　　　　　　　M Tu W Th F Sa Su

How is your wellness today?	UP	OK	DOWN
EMOTIONAL			
PHYSICAL			
SPIRITUAL			
INTELLECTUAL			
ENVIRONMENTAL			
SOCIAL			
OCCUPATIONAL			
FINANCIAL			

How have you improved your wellness today?

What are your wellness plans for tomorrow?

Name one positive from today

Notes

Daily Reflection: Week Seven

Date　　　　　　　　　　　M Tu W Th F Sa Su

How is your wellness today?	UP	OK	DOWN
EMOTIONAL			
PHYSICAL			
SPIRITUAL			
INTELLECTUAL			
ENVIRONMENTAL			
SOCIAL			
OCCUPATIONAL			
FINANCIAL			

How have you improved your wellness today?

What are your wellness plans for tomorrow?

Name one positive from today

Notes

Daily Reflection: Week Seven

Date   M Tu W Th F Sa Su

How is your wellness today?	UP	OK	DOWN
EMOTIONAL			
PHYSICAL			
SPIRITUAL			
INTELLECTUAL			
ENVIRONMENTAL			
SOCIAL			
OCCUPATIONAL			
FINANCIAL			

How have you improved your wellness today?

What are your wellness plans for tomorrow?

Name one positive from today

Notes

Daily Reflection: Week Seven

Date　　　　　　　　　　　M　Tu　W　Th　F　Sa　Su

How is your wellness today?	UP	OK	DOWN
EMOTIONAL			
PHYSICAL			
SPIRITUAL			
INTELLECTUAL			
ENVIRONMENTAL			
SOCIAL			
OCCUPATIONAL			
FINANCIAL			

How have you improved your wellness today?

What are your wellness plans for tomorrow?

Name one positive from today

Notes

Daily Reflection: Week Eight

Date M Tu W Th F Sa Su

How is your wellness today?	UP	OK	DOWN
EMOTIONAL			
PHYSICAL			
SPIRITUAL			
INTELLECTUAL			
ENVIRONMENTAL			
SOCIAL			
OCCUPATIONAL			
FINANCIAL			

How have you improved your wellness today?

What are your wellness plans for tomorrow?

Name one positive from today

Notes

Daily Reflection: Week Eight

Date   M Tu W Th F Sa Su

How is your wellness today?	UP	OK	DOWN
EMOTIONAL			
PHYSICAL			
SPIRITUAL			
INTELLECTUAL			
ENVIRONMENTAL			
SOCIAL			
OCCUPATIONAL			
FINANCIAL			

How have you improved your wellness today?

What are your wellness plans for tomorrow?

Name one positive from today

Notes

Daily Reflection: Week Eight

Date   M   Tu   W   Th   F   Sa   Su

How is your wellness today?	UP	OK	DOWN
EMOTIONAL			
PHYSICAL			
SPIRITUAL			
INTELLECTUAL			
ENVIRONMENTAL			
SOCIAL			
OCCUPATIONAL			
FINANCIAL			

How have you improved your wellness today?

What are your wellness plans for tomorrow?

Name one positive from today

Notes

Daily Reflection: Week Eight

Date M Tu W Th F Sa Su

How is your wellness today?	UP	OK	DOWN
EMOTIONAL			
PHYSICAL			
SPIRITUAL			
INTELLECTUAL			
ENVIRONMENTAL			
SOCIAL			
OCCUPATIONAL			
FINANCIAL			

How have you improved your wellness today?

What are your wellness plans for tomorrow?

Name one positive from today

Notes

Daily Reflection: Week Eight

Date M Tu W Th F Sa Su

How is your wellness today?	UP	OK	DOWN
EMOTIONAL			
PHYSICAL			
SPIRITUAL			
INTELLECTUAL			
ENVIRONMENTAL			
SOCIAL			
OCCUPATIONAL			
FINANCIAL			

How have you improved your wellness today?

What are your wellness plans for tomorrow?

Name one positive from today

Notes

Daily Reflection: Week Eight

Date 　　　　　　　　M Tu W Th F Sa Su

How is your wellness today?	UP	OK	DOWN
EMOTIONAL			
PHYSICAL			
SPIRITUAL			
INTELLECTUAL			
ENVIRONMENTAL			
SOCIAL			
OCCUPATIONAL			
FINANCIAL			

How have you improved your wellness today?

What are your wellness plans for tomorrow?

Name one positive from today

Notes

Daily Reflection: Week Eight

Date　　　　　　　　　　M　Tu　W　Th　F　Sa　Su

How is your wellness today?	UP	OK	DOWN
EMOTIONAL			
PHYSICAL			
SPIRITUAL			
INTELLECTUAL			
ENVIRONMENTAL			
SOCIAL			
OCCUPATIONAL			
FINANCIAL			

How have you improved your wellness today?

What are your wellness plans for tomorrow?

Name one positive from today

Month Two Review

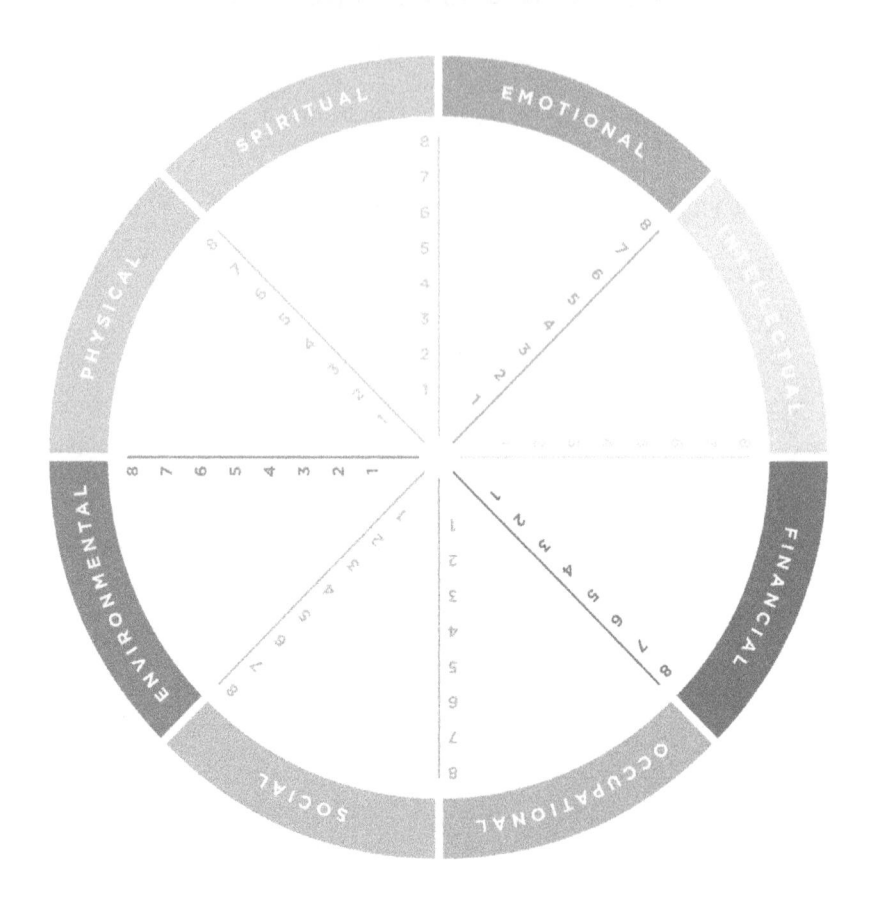

Reassess yourself against the eight wellness elements. Have there been any changes?

Month Two Self Reflection

What went well this month?

What did not go well this month?

What have you learnt from the past month?

Review your goals
(goals can be changed and adapted if need be)

	On Track	On Hold	Problem
SHORT TERM GOAL			
MIDTERM GOAL			
LONG TERM GOAL			

Environmental Wellness Tips

1 **Declutter**
Decluttering your space can help declutter our mind. Start one space at a time.

2 **Get outside**
Enjoying nature helps reduce stress, increase endorphins, and lets you appreciate the world around you.

3 **Bring the outdors inside**
Plants can improve indoor air quality fresh air improves sleep. A dose of nature can enhance energy and performance.

4 **Environmentally Friendly**
Ditching unnecessary chemicals, unhealthy foods, unfriendly eco practices, and bad habits/routines will improve health the environment and ecosystem

5 **Know your preferred environment**
Know the environment that bring out the best in you and spend regular, quality time in them.

Social Wellness Tips

1 **Reflection**
Reflect on yourself and your social needs. What parts of your social life do you enjoy? What parts would you like to improve?

2 **Support System**
Take time to identify who your support systems are, the people who you share a 50/50 relationship with

3 **Keep in touch**
Make time to keep in touch with the people in your support system. Keep those relationships strong.

4 **Boundaries**
Build healthy boundaries with people, they set the basic guidelines of how you want to be treated

5 **Say Goodbye**
Don't be scared of letting go of toxic relationships, how long someone has been in your life should not equate to how long you accept a negative relationship

Notes

Daily Reflection: Week Nine

Date M Tu W Th F Sa Su

How is your wellness today?	UP	OK	DOWN
EMOTIONAL			
PHYSICAL			
SPIRITUAL			
INTELLECTUAL			
ENVIRONMENTAL			
SOCIAL			
OCCUPATIONAL			
FINANCIAL			

How have you improved your wellness today?

What are your wellness plans for tomorrow?

Name one positive from today

Notes

Daily Reflection: Week Nine

Date M Tu W Th F Sa Su

How is your wellness today?	UP	OK	DOWN
EMOTIONAL			
PHYSICAL			
SPIRITUAL			
INTELLECTUAL			
ENVIRONMENTAL			
SOCIAL			
OCCUPATIONAL			
FINANCIAL			

How have you improved your wellness today?

What are your wellness plans for tomorrow?

Name one positive from today

Notes

Daily Reflection: Week Nine

Date M Tu W Th F Sa Su

How is your wellness today?	UP	OK	DOWN
EMOTIONAL			
PHYSICAL			
SPIRITUAL			
INTELLECTUAL			
ENVIRONMENTAL			
SOCIAL			
OCCUPATIONAL			
FINANCIAL			

How have you improved your wellness today?

What are your wellness plans for tomorrow?

Name one positive from today

Notes

Daily Reflection: Week Nine

Date M Tu W Th F Sa Su

How is your wellness today?	UP	OK	DOWN
EMOTIONAL			
PHYSICAL			
SPIRITUAL			
INTELLECTUAL			
ENVIRONMENTAL			
SOCIAL			
OCCUPATIONAL			
FINANCIAL			

How have you improved your wellness today?

What are your wellness plans for tomorrow?

Name one positive from today

Notes

Daily Reflection: Week Nine

Date　　　　　　　　　　M　Tu　W　Th　F　Sa　Su

How is your wellness today?	UP	OK	DOWN
EMOTIONAL			
PHYSICAL			
SPIRITUAL			
INTELLECTUAL			
ENVIRONMENTAL			
SOCIAL			
OCCUPATIONAL			
FINANCIAL			

How have you improved your wellness today?

What are your wellness plans for tomorrow?

Name one positive from today

Notes

Daily Reflection: Week Nine

Date　　　　　　　　　　　M Tu W Th F Sa Su

How is your wellness today?	UP	OK	DOWN
EMOTIONAL			
PHYSICAL			
SPIRITUAL			
INTELLECTUAL			
ENVIRONMENTAL			
SOCIAL			
OCCUPATIONAL			
FINANCIAL			

How have you improved your wellness today?

What are your wellness plans for tomorrow?

Name one positive from today

Notes

Daily Reflection: Week Nine

Date　　　　　　　　　　M Tu W Th F Sa Su

How is your wellness today?	UP	OK	DOWN
EMOTIONAL			
PHYSICAL			
SPIRITUAL			
INTELLECTUAL			
ENVIRONMENTAL			
SOCIAL			
OCCUPATIONAL			
FINANCIAL			

How have you improved your wellness today?

What are your wellness plans for tomorrow?

Name one positive from today

Notes

Daily Reflection: Week Ten

Date　　　　　　　　　　M　Tu　W　Th　F　Sa　Su

How is your wellness today?	UP	OK	DOWN
EMOTIONAL			
PHYSICAL			
SPIRITUAL			
INTELLECTUAL			
ENVIRONMENTAL			
SOCIAL			
OCCUPATIONAL			
FINANCIAL			

How have you improved your wellness today?

What are your wellness plans for tomorrow?

Name one positive from today

Notes

Daily Reflection: Week Ten

Date M Tu W Th F Sa Su

How is your wellness today?	UP	OK	DOWN
EMOTIONAL			
PHYSICAL			
SPIRITUAL			
INTELLECTUAL			
ENVIRONMENTAL			
SOCIAL			
OCCUPATIONAL			
FINANCIAL			

How have you improved your wellness today?

What are your wellness plans for tomorrow?

Name one positive from today

Notes

Daily Reflection: Week Ten

Date M Tu W Th F Sa Su

How is your wellness today?	UP	OK	DOWN
EMOTIONAL			
PHYSICAL			
SPIRITUAL			
INTELLECTUAL			
ENVIRONMENTAL			
SOCIAL			
OCCUPATIONAL			
FINANCIAL			

How have you improved your wellness today?

What are your wellness plans for tomorrow?

Name one positive from today

Notes

Daily Reflection: Week Ten

Date　　　　　　　　　　　M　Tu　W　Th　F　Sa　Su

How is your wellness today?	UP	OK	DOWN
EMOTIONAL			
PHYSICAL			
SPIRITUAL			
INTELLECTUAL			
ENVIRONMENTAL			
SOCIAL			
OCCUPATIONAL			
FINANCIAL			

How have you improved your wellness today?

What are your wellness plans for tomorrow?

Name one positive from today

Notes

Daily Reflection: Week Ten

Date   M   Tu   W   Th   F   Sa   Su

How is your wellness today?	UP	OK	DOWN
EMOTIONAL			
PHYSICAL			
SPIRITUAL			
INTELLECTUAL			
ENVIRONMENTAL			
SOCIAL			
OCCUPATIONAL			
FINANCIAL			

How have you improved your wellness today?

What are your wellness plans for tomorrow?

Name one positive from today

Notes

Daily Reflection: Week Ten

Date   M   Tu   W   Th   F   Sa   Su

How is your wellness today?	UP	OK	DOWN
EMOTIONAL			
PHYSICAL			
SPIRITUAL			
INTELLECTUAL			
ENVIRONMENTAL			
SOCIAL			
OCCUPATIONAL			
FINANCIAL			

How have you improved your wellness today?

What are your wellness plans for tomorrow?

Name one positive from today

Notes

Daily Reflection: Week Ten

Date M Tu W Th F Sa Su

How is your wellness today?	UP	OK	DOWN
EMOTIONAL			
PHYSICAL			
SPIRITUAL			
INTELLECTUAL			
ENVIRONMENTAL			
SOCIAL			
OCCUPATIONAL			
FINANCIAL			

How have you improved your wellness today?

What are your wellness plans for tomorrow?

Name one positive from today

Notes

Daily Reflection: Week Eleven

Date M Tu W Th F Sa Su

How is your wellness today?	UP	OK	DOWN
EMOTIONAL			
PHYSICAL			
SPIRITUAL			
INTELLECTUAL			
ENVIRONMENTAL			
SOCIAL			
OCCUPATIONAL			
FINANCIAL			

How have you improved your wellness today?

What are your wellness plans for tomorrow?

Name one positive from today

Notes

Daily Reflection: Week Eleven

Date _____ M Tu W Th F Sa Su

How is your wellness today?	UP	OK	DOWN
EMOTIONAL			
PHYSICAL			
SPIRITUAL			
INTELLECTUAL			
ENVIRONMENTAL			
SOCIAL			
OCCUPATIONAL			
FINANCIAL			

How have you improved your wellness today?

What are your wellness plans for tomorrow?

Name one positive from today

Notes

Daily Reflection: Week Eleven

Date   M   Tu   W   Th   F   Sa   Su

How is your wellness today?	UP	OK	DOWN
EMOTIONAL			
PHYSICAL			
SPIRITUAL			
INTELLECTUAL			
ENVIRONMENTAL			
SOCIAL			
OCCUPATIONAL			
FINANCIAL			

How have you improved your wellness today?

What are your wellness plans for tomorrow?

Name one positive from today

Notes

Daily Reflection: Week Eleven

Date _____ M Tu W Th F Sa Su

How is your wellness today?	UP	OK	DOWN
EMOTIONAL			
PHYSICAL			
SPIRITUAL			
INTELLECTUAL			
ENVIRONMENTAL			
SOCIAL			
OCCUPATIONAL			
FINANCIAL			

How have you improved your wellness today?

What are your wellness plans for tomorrow?

Name one positive from today

Notes

Daily Reflection: Week Eleven

Date _____ M Tu W Th F Sa Su

How is your wellness today?	UP	OK	DOWN
EMOTIONAL			
PHYSICAL			
SPIRITUAL			
INTELLECTUAL			
ENVIRONMENTAL			
SOCIAL			
OCCUPATIONAL			
FINANCIAL			

How have you improved your wellness today?

What are your wellness plans for tomorrow?

Name one positive from today

Notes

Daily Reflection: Week Eleven

Date _____ M Tu W Th F Sa Su

How is your wellness today?	UP	OK	DOWN
EMOTIONAL			
PHYSICAL			
SPIRITUAL			
INTELLECTUAL			
ENVIRONMENTAL			
SOCIAL			
OCCUPATIONAL			
FINANCIAL			

How have you improved your wellness today?

What are your wellness plans for tomorrow?

Name one positive from today

Notes

Daily Reflection: Week Eleven

Date M Tu W Th F Sa Su

How is your wellness today?	UP	OK	DOWN
EMOTIONAL			
PHYSICAL			
SPIRITUAL			
INTELLECTUAL			
ENVIRONMENTAL			
SOCIAL			
OCCUPATIONAL			
FINANCIAL			

How have you improved your wellness today?

What are your wellness plans for tomorrow?

Name one positive from today

Notes

Daily Reflection: Week Twelve

Date   M   Tu   W   Th   F   Sa   Su

How is your wellness today?	UP	OK	DOWN
EMOTIONAL			
PHYSICAL			
SPIRITUAL			
INTELLECTUAL			
ENVIRONMENTAL			
SOCIAL			
OCCUPATIONAL			
FINANCIAL			

How have you improved your wellness today?

What are your wellness plans for tomorrow?

Name one positive from today

Notes

Daily Reflection: Week Twelve

Date M Tu W Th F Sa Su

How is your wellness today?	UP	OK	DOWN
EMOTIONAL			
PHYSICAL			
SPIRITUAL			
INTELLECTUAL			
ENVIRONMENTAL			
SOCIAL			
OCCUPATIONAL			
FINANCIAL			

How have you improved your wellness today?

What are your wellness plans for tomorrow?

Name one positive from today

Notes

Daily Reflection: Week Twelve

Date M Tu W Th F Sa Su

How is your wellness today?	UP	OK	DOWN
EMOTIONAL			
PHYSICAL			
SPIRITUAL			
INTELLECTUAL			
ENVIRONMENTAL			
SOCIAL			
OCCUPATIONAL			
FINANCIAL			

How have you improved your wellness today?

What are your wellness plans for tomorrow?

Name one positive from today

Notes

Daily Reflection: Week Twelve

Date   M   Tu   W   Th   F   Sa   Su

How is your wellness today?	UP	OK	DOWN
EMOTIONAL			
PHYSICAL			
SPIRITUAL			
INTELLECTUAL			
ENVIRONMENTAL			
SOCIAL			
OCCUPATIONAL			
FINANCIAL			

How have you improved your wellness today?

What are your wellness plans for tomorrow?

Name one positive from today

Notes

Daily Reflection: Week Twelve

Date   M Tu W Th F Sa Su

How is your wellness today?	UP	OK	DOWN
EMOTIONAL			
PHYSICAL			
SPIRITUAL			
INTELLECTUAL			
ENVIRONMENTAL			
SOCIAL			
OCCUPATIONAL			
FINANCIAL			

How have you improved your wellness today?

What are your wellness plans for tomorrow?

Name one positive from today

Notes

Daily Reflection: Week Twelve

Date   M   Tu   W   Th   F   Sa   Su

How is your wellness today?	UP	OK	DOWN
EMOTIONAL			
PHYSICAL			
SPIRITUAL			
INTELLECTUAL			
ENVIRONMENTAL			
SOCIAL			
OCCUPATIONAL			
FINANCIAL			

How have you improved your wellness today?

What are your wellness plans for tomorrow?

Name one positive from today

Notes

Daily Reflection: Week Twelve

Date M Tu W Th F Sa Su

How is your wellness today?	UP	OK	DOWN
EMOTIONAL			
PHYSICAL			
SPIRITUAL			
INTELLECTUAL			
ENVIRONMENTAL			
SOCIAL			
OCCUPATIONAL			
FINANCIAL			

How have you improved your wellness today?

What are your wellness plans for tomorrow?

Name one positive from today

Month Three Review

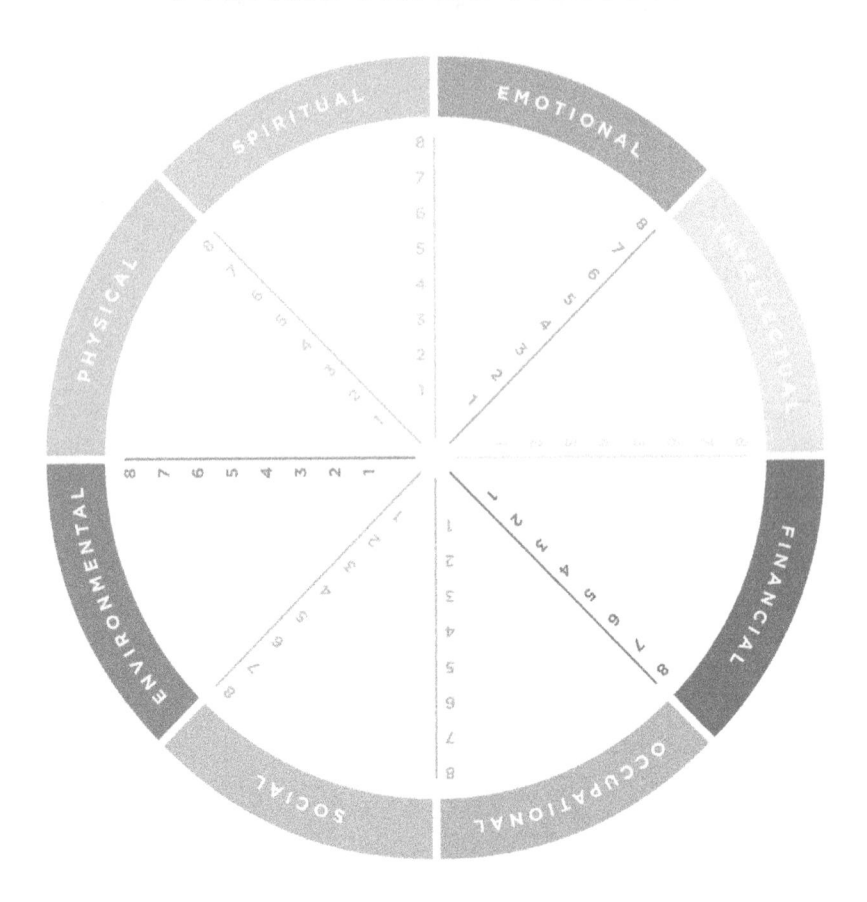

Reassess yourself against the eight wellness elements. Have there been any changes?

Month Three Self Reflection

What went well this month?

What did not go well this month?

What have you learnt from the past month?

Review your goals (goals can be changed and adapted if need be)	On Track	On Hold	Problem
SHORT TERM GOAL			
MIDTERM GOAL			
LONG TERM GOAL			

Your 8Wise™ Wellness Journey

What have you enjoyed most about the past 12 weeks?

What has surprised you most?

How did your goals go?

Better than expected	
Exactly what I wanted	
They were unrealistic	
I did not stick to my plans	

What have you learnt from the past month?

Occupational Wellness Tips

1 **Work life balance**
Manage the waves of responsibility realistically and not choosing to only exist in one area of your life

2 **Don't settle**
Continue to set goals and work towards them whether it be with current employer, your current role or your current career.

3 **Develop**
Find ways to increase knowledge and skills to keep you motivated, interested and stimulated.

4 **Benefits**
Identify and focus on the benefits to your current role/career. If you're struggling with this, then make changes.

5 **Say Goodbye**
Don't be scared of moving on. Look for something new and/or talk to a career counsellor if you feel stuck or unhappy

Financial Wellness Tips

1 **Relationship with money**
Reflect on what money really means to you, and how it supports your values, beliefs and purpose.

2 **Financial literacy**
Develop financial literacy, knowledge and skills to make effective decisions and develop money management tools

3 **Financial planning**
Identify your current financial situation, create clear goals for where you want your finances to be and why.

4 **Money managment**
Track your monthly income and expenditure through a budget that is in a format of your choice and is user friendly for you.

5 **Say Goodbye to the credit cycle**
Understand credit/debt cycle traps and their effects on credit scoring. Make small changes towards breaking the cycle.

"The relationships and support systems we build help us navigate our lives, in good times and in bad. It is important to establish positive and regular interactions with them."

For more support, tips and information about 8Wise™ please follow us:

Daltonwise.co.uk

@8wisekim
@daltonwsiecoaching

@8wise
@daltonwisecoachingandtherapy

@8Wise_Kim
@daltonWiseCoach

https://www.linkedin.com/company/dalton-wise-coaching-and-therapy

https://www.pinterest.co.uk/daltonwiseltd/

About the Author

Who better to be your 8Wise™ guide than its creator, Kim Rutherford, Co-founder of Dalton Wise Ltd, a mental health and wellness support service. Mental health has been a part of Kim's life since her childhood, it's what inspired her to become a psychotherapist and mental wellness coach, trainer and corporate consultant.

She is based in Liverpool, England where she uses 8Wise™ to help her clients take back control of their mental wellness and protect their longer term mental health.